LITTLE VIOLET AND THE ANGEL

First published in 2001 by Oberon Books Ltd.

521 Caledonian Road, London N7 9RH

Tel: +44 (0) 20 7607 3637 / Fax: +44 (0) 20 7607 3629

e-mail: info@oberonbooks.com

www.oberonbooks.com

A catalogue record for this book is available from the British Library.

ISBN: 978-1-84002-217-9

Cover artwork: © Kean Lanyon

Series design: Richard Doust

Visit www.oberonbooks.com to read more about all our books and to buy them. You will also find features, author interviews and news of any author events, and you can sign up for e-newsletters so that you're always first to hear about our new releases.

Characters

GABRIEL
a young angel

ANA-MARIA

A GIRL/MOTHER
a young woman of gypsy or Turkish parentage

VLAD
Ana-Maria's husband

VIORICA
a baby then a little girl

WOMAN

DOCTOR

ARCHANGEL GABRIEL

BEAR

BEAR CUB

SINGER

Viorica is portrayed by several puppets which get bigger as the play progresses.

Bear and Bear Cub are to be portrayed by puppets or projections or actors at the director's and designer's discretion.

The play is set in Romania and the music should have a distinct Balkan flavour – the original music by Liviu Manolache is available on cassette from the writer's agent.

Pronunciation: Viorica (Vee-or-reek-a) with the stress on the second "i".

'Puişor, măi puişor' means 'Little chick, oh little chick' and is pronounced *pweeshor, my pweeshor* with the stress on the second syllable of 'puişor'.

Earth

RED.

A baby is born. The SINGER and the PUPPETEERS rush around with pans of water. There is much commotion and shouting accompanied by the sounds made by tins whistles, saucepans etc.

They form the baby out of the sheet.

A baby cries.

They try to calm it.

The SINGER plays some music.

Everything turns WHITE.

The baby stops crying.

A feather flutters down. They look up.

Heaven

BLUE.

GABRIEL: Gabriel's the name.
    I'm an angel you know.
    Like my wings?
    Bit small, aren't they?
    They're not proper ones.
    I haven't earned my proper ones yet.
    I've just arrived you see.
    Apparently I used to live down there.

He looks down.

Whoa!
I hate heights.

He looks down again.

Whoooahoooah.
Long way down isn't it?
Funny thing is
I don't remember a thing about being down there.
No-one ever does.
I just woke up surrounded by all these clouds and
celestial beings.
They gave me this harp as well
But I'm not sure how to play it
I think it needs tuning
Because when I try and play a song on it
It sounds dreadful.

He plays a discordant note.

He just gave it me, the boss.
I said, 'I don't know how to play the harp.'
He said, 'You'll learn.'

He tries to play again. It sounds even worse.

His name's Gabriel too.
The one who gave me the harp,
My boss.
But he's the big cheese.
He's what you call an archangel.
You should see the wings on him.
They're massive!
I'm just a common angel.
In the scheme of things
I'm not much higher than a cherub.
In fact he was quite upset,
The other Gabriel, I mean,
I suppose he didn't want to be sharing his name with
        somebody as low down the pecking order as me.
Anyway
I haven't got time to dawdle talking to you.
Got work to do,

Places to go,
People to see.
I'm looking for a little girl.
I'm supposed to be her guardian angel.
I have to watch over her.
It's my first job.
He said,
If I do it well,
Then I might get wings like his.
Perhaps you've seen her. Have you?
He gave me a description
My boss,
The other Gabriel.
Hang on.

He gets out a piece of paper and reads.

Two eyes…

He looks at the audience.

Hmmm.

He reads the paper again.

A nose…

He looks at the audience.

Mmmm.

Reads the paper.

A mouth…

He looks at the audience.

Mmmmm.
Giggles when she's tickled.
You!
Do you giggle when you're tickled?
Mmmm.

And do you?
Who else giggles when they're tickled?
Oh,
Lots of you.

He reads.

Forty centimetres long.

The SINGER gives him a ruler and GABRIEL tries to measure out forty centimetres. It is difficult because the ruler is only thirty centimetres. Eventually he manages to do it against his leg. He is shocked at how small the little girl is.

I didn't know they came that small.

He puts his hand forty centimetres from the ground and looks into the audience to see if any of the children out there are that small. He is very confused. He looks at the other side of the paper.

Wait a minute.
It says here she's a baby.
A baby?
I can't quite remember what that is.
A baby…
It's um…
Isn't it one of those…?
Don't tell me!
A baby?
Is it an animal?
No? What colour is it?
Can you eat it?
No?
Mmmm?
What?

The audience tell him what a baby is. He is very slow to understand.

So I've got to look for a little girl with no hair who cries a lot and who sicks her dinner down her dress all the time. (Or *whatever* the audience have said.)

Hang on there's more.
She lives in a far-away country –
Oh dear.
I don't think this is going to be very easy.

– a far-away country where there are still bears in the forests and wolves in the mountains and her mother is very very poor.

Mmmm.

He looks up to think and then looks at the paper again and jumps in fright.

Wolves!
Bears!
I remember them!
They're those…

He mimes a snarling wolf.

Those…

He mimes a bear rising on its hind legs.

Those…

He gnashes his teeth ferociously.

Yikes!
Don't like the sound of this.
A far-away country…
How am I going to get there?
Mmmm?
Fly!
I can't fly!
What with?
My what?

My wings?
Oh.

He looks at his wings.

I forgot about them.
The boss told me that's what they were for.
Flying.
Wait a minute, wait a minute!
I can't fly with these.
Look at them!
Would you trust these little things?

He tries to flap his wings.

See! Hopeless.

He tries again. This time he starts to rise a bit.

Wowohhhh.
That was funny.

He tries to flap his wings again. He lifts slowly off the ground.

You see this?
You see?
I'm flying.
I'm flying.

He looks down. And comes to the ground with a bump.

Oh yes.
He told me not to look down.
Forgot about that.

He tries to fly again. He lifts off the ground. He starts to look down and almost crashes again but remembers just in time.

Right.
Here we go.
And don't forget if you see one of those baby things

Let me know.

He flies off.

FLIGHT SEQUENCE. An ANGEL flies through the sky, past clouds and birds and aeroplanes. A little BOY looks out of the window of the aeroplane but when his MOTHER looks the ANGEL disappears.

SINGER: (*Sings.*)

IF YOU LOOK IN THE SKY
ON A STARRY NIGHT
YOU MIGHT SEE A LIGHT
WAY UP HIGH
IT MIGHT BE A PLANE
OR IT MIGHT BE A STAR
OR EVEN A SPACE SHIP
COMING FROM AFAR.
BUT IF YOU'RE REALLY LUCKY
YOU MIGHT SEE WINGS
A HALO AND A HARP
AND OTHER SUCH THINGS
AND IF YOU DO
DON'T RUB YOUR EYES
IT'S AN ANGEL FLYING
ACROSS THE SKIES.
AN ANGEL LOOKING
FOR SOME POOR LOST SOUL
OR LOOKING FOR A CHILD
WITH NO PLACE TO GO.
SO BLOW HIM A KISS
AND SAY, 'HAVE A GOOD FLIGHT!
I HOPE YOU FIND
THAT CHILD TONIGHT.'

Earth

A GIRL enters with a bundle. She tickles it and the baby laughs.

She lays the baby on the doorstep. She takes a chain from her neck on which there is a ring. She puts the chain around the baby's neck, kisses it. She sings.

> PUIŞOR, MĂI PUIŞOR,
> ONE AND ONE MAKE TWO
> PUIŞOR, MĂI PUIŞOR,
> THERE'S A HOLE IN MY SHOE.
> PUIŞOR, MĂI PUIŞOR,
> TWO AND TWO MAKE FOUR
> PUIŞOR, MĂI PUIŞOR,
> KNOCK, KNOCK, KNOCK ON THE DOOR.

She knocks on the door.

> PUIŞOR, MĂI PUIŞOR,
> FOUR AND FOUR MAKE EIGHT
> PUIŞOR, MĂI PUIŞOR,
> IT'S GETTING VERY LATE.
> THE WIND WILL SING A LULLABY
> THE MOON WILL LIGHT YOUR WAY
> THE SNOW WILL BE YOUR BLANKET
> WHEN I'M FAR FAR AWAY

She knocks on the door again. Listens and hears no response. Relieved, she picks up the baby and is about to go away when she hears footsteps. She kisses the baby and puts it down again. She hides and watches.

Inside the house

ANA-MARIA is looking at a photograph album.

ANA-MARIA: Vlad!

VLAD: Yes, my love?

ANA-MARIA: Where are you going?

VLAD: There was a knock on the door.

He continues towards the door.

ANA-MARIA: Vlad!

VLAD: Yes, my darling?

ANA-MARIA: I'm cold, the wind is whistling through the gap in the window.

VLAD returns and wraps a blanket around her. He goes again.

Vlad!

VLAD: Yes, my sweet?

ANA-MARIA: My throat is so dry.

VLAD returns and pours her some milk.

Thank you.

She sips her milk. VLAD goes again.

Vlad?

VLAD: Yes, my dear?

ANA-MARIA: I thought a little biscuit...

VLAD: Of course, dear heart.

He returns and hands her a biscuit.

ANA-MARIA: Thank you.

He starts to go again and she clasps his hand.

Don't open the door at this time of night. There's no knowing who might be out there. It might be a burglar.

VLAD: It won't be a burglar.

ANA-MARIA: You can't be too careful.

VLAD: Ana-Maria, we can't live like this.

ANA-MARIA: But what if – ?

VLAD: Let me answer the door.

He goes to the door. There is no-one there. He starts to go. There is a baby's faint cry. He looks to the right and sees nothing. Starts to go again. Again there is a faint cry. He looks left. Nothing. He starts to leave again. Again there is a cry. He looks up. Still nothing. He starts to go inside and again there is a cry. He goes back and this time he sees the baby.

What have we here?

ANA-MARIA: What is it?

VLAD: Hello.

ANA-MARIA: Vlad!

VLAD: Where did you come from?

ANA-MARIA: Vlad!

VLAD picks up the baby.

Vlad, are you alright?

She gets up and comes to the door.

He turns.

What is it?

VLAD: A baby.

ANA-MARIA: A baby?

VLAD: A little baby.

He goes into the room and sits holding the baby. ANA-MARIA looks on as he gently feeds it milk on his finger.

GABRIEL enters.

GABRIEL: I knew this wasn't going to be easy.
She's ended up with those two old fossils.

Those two old gargoyles.
Those two old –
Look at the face on him!
Looks like something from a horror film.
And did you hear her?
'Vlad, I'm cold.'
'Vlad!'
'My throat's dry.'
'Vlad!'
'I thought a little biscuit.' She doesn't look the sort
who'd tickle a baby.

He looks around.

What is this place anyway?
I could swear…
I'm sure…
This house, it feels like…
It feels like I've been here before.
I wonder if that's normal.
Have to ask the boss.

VLAD: What's that you've got round your neck? It's a gold
chain.

ANA-MARIA looks up.

And there's a ring on it. With a pretty purple stone.

ANA-MARIA: What are you going to do?

VLAD: What do you mean?

He gives the baby his finger to suck.

Do you like that, my little cherub? She's hungry, poor
little thing.

ANA-MARIA: We'll have to talk to the people at the
orphanage.

VLAD: What for?

ANA-MARIA: What do you mean, 'What for?'

VLAD: I mean why?

ANA-MARIA: They'll look after it.

VLAD: We can look after it.

ANA-MARIA: Don't be ridiculous. We can't look after a baby.

VLAD: We did once before.

ANA-MARIA: What?

VLAD: I just mean –

ANA-MARIA: You think this, this thing, could ever take my Gaby's place?

VLAD: I wasn't saying –

ANA-MARIA: How could you even…? Nothing could ever replace Gaby in my heart. You hear me? When he died the light went out of my life. For ever. Look at him!

She holds out the album.

VLAD: Ana-Maria, please!

ANA-MARIA: You never want to look at his photos.

VLAD: I can't.

ANA-MARIA: Such a beautiful baby. He was just six months old in this photo. Already you could see how handsome he was going to be. Such a handsome boy. Such a handsome man. Look at him, there he is playing his violin at the school concert. And that's one we took before he went to the airport. That's the last time we ever saw him.

VLAD: Please, Ana-Maria.

GABRIEL goes to look at the photo album but just as he is about to do so ANA-MARIA closes it.

ANA-MARIA: And then you talk to me about taking in some urchin from the streets, some squawking beggar's child. You never loved him like I did.

VLAD: Ana-Maria, that's not true.

ANA-MARIA: My poor Gaby. My poor boy.

She cries.

VLAD: We have to take her in. We can't leave her out in the snow.

VLAD goes to heat the baby some milk.

ANA-MARIA rocks herself in her chair. ANA-MARIA holds the album like a baby. GABRIEL goes and looks at her. She doesn't see him. He waves his hand in front of her eyes. She doesn't respond. GABRIEL looks at the audience and grins. He pulls a face at ANA-MARIA. Still no response. He waggles his hand by his ears and pokes his tongue out. Again, no response. He flaps his wings at her. ANA-MARIA shivers and pulls the blanket round her.

ANA-MARIA: Freezing cold in here. Vlad! Have you left that door open?

GABRIEL: Well, there's not a lot more to be done here. Looks like my little girl is going to be alright tonight.

He starts to go.

ANA-MARIA: Vlad! Make sure that door's locked. Someone said they saw a bear in the street last night.

GABRIEL freezes in horror.

They come sniffing around the dustbins
Looking for food.

GABRIEL: Yikes!

SINGER: (*Sings.*)

THERE'S A BABY IN THE HOUSE
SO DON'T BANG THE DOOR!
DON'T SCRAPE THE CHAIR LEGS
ALONG THE FLOOR.
A BABY NEEDS QUIET
AND A BABY NEEDS SLEEP
SO TIPTOE DOWN THE STAIRS
AND DON'T STAMP YOUR FEET.

THERE'S A BABY IN THE HOUSE
KEEP THE DOG IN HIS PLACE
AND DON'T LET THE CAT
GO ON LIE ON BABY'S FACE.
BECAUSE THEY MIGHT GET JEALOUS
AND THEY MIGHT BEGIN TO POUT
IF WE MAKE A FUSS OF BABY
AND LEAVE THEM OUT.

THERE'S A BABY IN THE HOUSE
HOW MANY BLANKETS IN THE COT?
SHE MUSTN'T GET TOO COLD
AND SHE MUSTN'T GET TOO HOT.
AND DON'T GET CROSS WITH BABY
IF SHE CRIES ALL NIGHT
AND ONLY GOES TO SLEEP
WITH THE MORNING LIGHT.

THERE'S A BABY IN THE HOUSE
AND SHE'S WATCHING YOU
BABY SEES AND HEARS
EVERYTHING YOU DO.
SO ALWAYS REMEMBER
TO WATCH WHAT YOU SAY.
EVERYTHING YOU GIVE
SHE'LL GIVE YOU BACK ONE DAY.

BABY GETTING BIGGER SEQUENCE. During the song we see VLAD tend the baby. He holds her and realises that she is damp and that she needs her nappy changing. He tries to do it and is knocked back by the smell. ANA-MARIA watches balefully. She is looking through the album.

VLAD puts the baby in a cot. He hears her cry and returns to the cot. The baby is bigger. He puts her on the floor and she can now crawl. She is naughty and he has to keep stopping her get up to mischief. She keeps trying to pester ANA-MARIA. VLAD has to keep trying to distract her.

ANA-MARIA: You see. You can't look after a baby.

VLAD: Come here, little one.

ANA-MARIA: You're old, Vlad.

VLAD: Not too old.

ANA-MARIA: Not yet perhaps. But what happens when you're not here any more?

VLAD: I've got a good few years in me yet.

ANA-MARIA: She'll be left on her own with nobody to look after her. Much better if you put her in an orphanage now. She'll have other children to play with. She needs other children.

VLAD: She likes it here. Don't you, my darling? If you're very good Ana-Maria will sing you one of her songs.

ANA-MARIA: I will not.

VLAD: Your beautiful voice.

ANA-MARIA: You're selfish, you know that?

VLAD: Selfish?

ANA-MARIA: Keeping her here because you miss our Gaby.

VLAD: I...

ANA-MARIA: She can't take his place.

She goes.

Heaven

GABRIEL: You know what I really like about being up here?
Playing hide and seek in the clouds.
It's fantastic.
You find this really dark rain-cloud
That nobody can see through,
You know a really big black cloud
And you dive right into the middle of it
And nobody can find you.

ARCHANGEL GABRIEL: Gabriel!

GABRIEL looks up.

GABRIEL: (*Whispering to the audience.*) You have to keep really still and quiet though.

ARCHANGEL GABRIEL: Gabriel! I know you're in there.

GABRIEL: Oh, fiddle my feathers!

ARCHANGEL GABRIEL: Come on, Gabriel! I've got something to ask you, Gabriel.

GABRIEL comes out of the cloud.

GABRIEL: What is it Mr Archangel Gabriel, Sir?

ARCHANGEL GABRIEL: Have you learnt to play your harp yet, Gabriel?

GABRIEL: I never seem to get the time.

ARCHANGEL GABRIEL: And when did you last see your little girl?

GABRIEL: Oh she's alright. I left her with those two old fogeys.

ARCHANGEL GABRIEL: Those two old fogeys, as you call them, are the people that she is supposed to be with. They're the people that are meant to be looking after her.

GABRIEL: Well, that's alright then, isn't it? If they're the people who are supposed to be looking after her then she doesn't need me. And to be quite honest, Mr Head Angel, Your Shiningness, I didn't really like the country she's living in. Do you know they've got wolves and bears there?

ARCHANGEL GABRIEL: Gabriel?

GABRIEL: Yes?

ARCHANGEL GABRIEL: When did you last see her?

GABRIEL: Well, I…

ARCHANGEL GABRIEL: When Gabriel?

GABRIEL: The night she got left on the doorstep.

ARCHANGEL GABRIEL: That was six months ago, Gabriel.

GABRIEL: I'm sure she's alright.

ARCHANGEL GABRIEL: It's just not good enough Gabriel! How do you expect to get wings like mine if you can't look after your little girl properly? She's in danger at this very moment, Gabriel.

GABRIEL: Danger?

ARCHANGEL GABRIEL: Yes.

GABRIEL: What sort of danger?

ARCHANGEL GABRIEL: Serious danger.

GABRIEL: You mean a bear or wolf sort of danger?

ARCHANGEL GABRIEL: Nothing like that.

GABRIEL: That's alright then.

ARCHANGEL GABRIEL: Go to her Gabriel. And
remember she has to stay with the old man and his wife.

GABRIEL: Yes Sir, O Heavenly One.

ARCHANGEL GABRIEL goes.

Just when I was having fun.
Honestly you might think this is a cushy job up here
Frolicking in the clouds.
Let me tell you,
It's not.

ARCHANGEL GABRIEL reappears.

ARCHANGEL GABRIEL: Hurry up, Gabriel. And don't
forget to practice your harp.

GABRIEL looks at the children for sympathy and goes.

Earth

VLAD is putting on the baby's coat.

VLAD: There you are, my dear,
We're going to go for a little ride in the pushchair.

ANA-MARIA hands him the bottle.

ANA-MARIA: Don't forget this.

GABRIEL enters.

GABRIEL: Awhhh, he's going to take her for a walk. How nice.

ANA-MARIA: Here's her gloves.

VLAD: It's not that far to the orphanage.

GABRIEL: You what?

ANA-MARIA: You don't want to leave anything behind.

GABRIEL: To the where?

VLAD: I'll just…

ANA-MARIA: What are you looking for?

VLAD: Her ring.

GABRIEL: To the orphanage?

VLAD gets the ring and stares at it.

ANA-MARIA: Hurry up, Vlad.

He puts the chain around the baby's neck.

VLAD: Those two little blue eyes, so trusting.

ANA-MARIA: Vlad!

VLAD: Gaby had blue eyes.

GABRIEL: He's taking her to the orphanage. That means she'll go there and I'll be in trouble with His Shiningness!

ANA-MARIA: Go on, Vlad.

She goes.

VLAD puts the baby down and wheels out the buggy.

He turns to get the baby and while he's doing that GABRIEL wheels it away again.

VLAD turns to put the baby in the buggy and it isn't where he left it. He puts the baby down and goes to wheel the buggy back. Meanwhile the baby has seen GABRIEL and goes to him. GABRIEL tries to shush her. VLAD turns back to get VIORICA and can't see her. While he is looking, GABRIEL folds up the push chair and then hides so that the baby can't see him and point to him.

VLAD finds the baby and turns round to find the buggy collapsed. He puts the baby down and turns back to open the buggy. While he is trying to put the buggy up the baby crawls off to and finds GABRIEL.

VLAD opens the buggy and looks for the baby. He turns back to the buggy to check on it just as GABRIEL is about to collapse it again. GABRIEL has to stop. VLAD goes and finds the baby. GABRIEL folds up the buggy.

VLAD turns. He is very perplexed. This time he tries to open the buggy while keeping hold of the baby. She keeps trying to get to GABRIEL. VLAD looks around in a puzzled fashion. He eventually manages to open the buggy and put the baby in it.

VLAD: Won't be long, my love.

VLAD pushes the buggy around the stage and GABRIEL blows at him to stop him. VLAD just does his coat up. The baby laughs at GABRIEL.

Why are you laughing, little one?

GABRIEL puts his fingers to his lips. The baby giggles.

What's funny?

GABRIEL shakes his head at the baby. She giggles again.

What am I going to do with you? Eh?

The WOMAN who runs the orphanage comes to greet VLAD.

WOMAN: And this is the child, is it? What a little darling. What lovely blue eyes. And you say she was just abandoned on your doorstep. Isn't it awful? Oh, this is the ring, is it? We'll have to keep that safe for her. Well, she'll be well looked after here I can assure you. All our children are very happy. You can see that for yourself. Now, here's a pen.

She hands VLAD a pen.

Now I'll get you a form to fill in.

She goes to get the form and while she does so GABRIEL tries to get the pen but VLAD picks it up. GABRIEL pulls a face at the baby and she laughs at him.

(*Giving VLAD the paper.*) She's a happy little thing, isn't she?

GABRIEL tries to get the paper but VLAD picks it up and starts reading it. The baby laughs again at GABRIEL.

Shall I hold her while you fill it out?

VLAD: Thank you.

She giggles as VLAD hands her over to the WOMAN. GABRIEL shakes his head furiously at the baby.

WOMAN: See she'll be fine.

GABRIEL pinches her and she starts to cry.

It's alright my darling.

The baby hollers.

Shhh, shhh, shhh, shhh.

VLAD: You'd better give her back.

The WOMAN hands the baby back and she stops crying immediately. VLAD holds her as he tries to fill out the form.

It says here, 'Child's name.'

WOMAN: Yes.

VLAD: She hasn't got a name.

WOMAN: Well you can just leave that blank. We'll give her a name.

VLAD: I see.

He looks at the baby.

Only...

WOMAN: Yes?

VLAD: I was thinking...

WOMAN: You were?

VLAD: A name's very important.

WOMAN: It is.

VLAD: Too important to be left to strangers, don't you think?

WOMAN: But you're a stranger as well, aren't you?

VLAD: I am?

WOMAN: You don't really know anything about her, do you?

VLAD looks down at the baby. The WOMAN looks at the form.

You haven't signed it.

She hands it back to VLAD. He picks up the pen and just as he is about to sign the paper GABRIEL flaps his wings and the piece of paper falls on the floor.

VLAD looks puzzled.

(*Picking up the form.*) Oh dear, it's got all dirty. I'll get you another one.

She turns and goes. VLAD looks at the baby. GABRIEL watches him.

VLAD: A name's a very important thing.

GABRIEL nods.

It stays with you all your life.

GABRIEL nods again.

What if they call you something that doesn't suit you?

GABRIEL looks very worried in agreement.

Come on, little one.

He puts the baby in the buggy and leaves.

The WOMAN returns with the form.

WOMAN: Here we are.

She stops and looks around.

Oh!

GABRIEL blows the form out of her hand and leaves.

VLAD returns to the house.

VLAD: She chose us, Ana-Maria.

ANA-MARIA: What?

VLAD: She came and found our doorstep. I think we were meant to have her.

ANA-MARIA opens the photo album. There are some photos on the table and she is choosing ones to stick in.

We picked some flowers for you on the way back.

He hands her a bunch of violets. ANA-MARIA ignores him.

The baby wants to smell the flowers. VLAD takes one and lets her smell it.

Do you like that my little cherub?

The child eats the flower.

Oh you mustn't eat it darling. They're not to eat.

ANA-MARIA looks up in disgust.

The child wants another flower.

Now, now, gentle.

He lets her smell the flower.

Again she eats it.

No, little one.

He takes the flower away from her and puts the rest out of the baby's reach.

(*To ANA-MARIA.*) My sweet.

No response.

My dove?

ANA-MARIA looks at him.

I've been thinking.

ANA-MARIA: What?

VLAD: She ought to have a name.

ANA-MARIA returns to her photos.

ANA-MARIA: How do you know she hasn't already got a
name?

VLAD: If she has, we don't know it.

*While they're talking the baby is trying to get to
the flowers. Possibly they are on the table with the
photographs. It has a tablecloth and she is pulling the
cloth so that the vase slowly comes towards her. VLAD
and ANA-MARIA are oblivious to this.*

We could call her Daniela, Cristina, Elena.

*ANA-MARIA looks at him crossly. He stops and she
returns to her album.*

Iuliana, Mariana, Diana.

*ANA-MARIA looks at him again. He stops. She returns
to her album.*

Andreea, Medeea –

*ANA-MARIA looks at him witheringly at this last
name.*

*The baby has nearly reached the flowers. She pulls the
tablecloth.*

*Suddenly ANA-MARIA becomes aware of what the
baby is doing.*

ANA-MARIA: Watch that child!

*The photos and vase all fall off the table and water goes
everywhere.*

My photos, she's ruined my photos.

The baby starts to cry.

Get her away from me.

She picks up her photos and tries to dry them.

VLAD: It's okay, my sweet. Shh, shh, shhh. You like the flowers, don't you?

He holds out a flower to the baby. She calms down.

That's a violet. A little Violet.

The baby gurgles and tries to eat the flower.

That's it.

ANA-MARIA: What?

VLAD: That's what we'll call you. Viorica! Little Violet. We'll call her Viorica!

ANA-MARIA: Call her what you like. Just keep her away from my photos.

She goes.

VLAD sings to the baby who gradually gets bigger.

VLAD: (*Sings.*)
VIORICA
VIORICA,
THE NIGHT WAS COLD
THE WIND WAS BLEAKER
WHEN I FOUND YOU
ON THE DOORSTEP
IN A BLANKET
LITTLE SQUEAKER.

GABRIEL comes and watches.

GABRIEL: He keeps sending me back to check up on her.
'Why?' I ask him,
She doesn't need me.
Look at her,
It's quite obvious the old man dotes on her.

VIORICA waves at him. GABRIEL puts his finger in front of his lips.

VLAD: (*Sings.*)
SOMEONE LEFT YOU
VIORICA
BUT NO-ONE WAS THERE
WHEN I WENT TO SEEK HER.
SO I TOOK YOU INSIDE
BEFORE YOU GOT WEAKER
AND GAVE YOU SOME MILK
MY VIORICA.

GABRIEL: Look how fast she's growing.
Can't believe it.

VIORICA waves at GABRIEL. GABRIEL hides.
VIORICA tries to see him.

VLAD: (*Sings.*)
VIORICA
VIORICA
YOUR TUMMY GOT ROUND
YOUR HAIR GOT SLEEKER.
NOW YOU'RE DRINKING
FROM A BEAKER
AND YOU ARE A
LITTLE SPEAKER.

VIORICA: Tatā, tatā.

VLAD: What my sweet one?

VIORICA: Man!

GABRIEL signs for her to keep quiet.

VLAD: What man?

VIORICA: (*Pointing at GABRIEL.*) Man.

VLAD looks around but can't see anything.

VLAD: There's no man there, darling.

VIORICA: Man!

GABRIEL: I'm off.

Got to report back to His Shiningness.

VLAD: (*Sings.*)

TIME IS PASSING

VIORICA.

HIGH IN THE FOREST

THERE'S A MOUNTAIN PEAK WHERE

BEAR CUBS PLAY WITH THEIR MOTHER

AND TWEAK HER.

ONE DAY WE'LL GO THERE

VIORICA.

GABRIEL: Just don't expect me to come there with you.

GABRIEL flies off.

VLAD goes and opens the door.

ANA-MARIA: Why are you opening the door, Vlad?

VLAD: Because the spring is coming, my treasure. Look how the sun is shining through the branches of the cherry tree in the garden, Viorica. Doesn't it make you want to sing like in the old days?

ANA-MARIA: Spring! What is Spring to me if my Gaby isn't here to share it with me?

VLAD: Ana-Maria…

ANA-MARIA: In my heart it will always be winter. You hear me?

VLAD: Come Viorica, come into the garden. Look at all the flowers.

VIORICA: Flowers.

VLAD: Yes, flowers. Soon the cherry tree itself will be covered in blossoms.

He points up and then starts his work in the garden.

ANA-MARIA watches through the window.

VIORICA: Look, tatā.

VLAD: What?

VIORICA: Look!

VLAD: That's a bird.

VIORICA: Bird!

VLAD: The birds fly in the sky.

VIORICA: Why?

VLAD: What do you mean, 'Why?'

VIORICA: Why they fly in the sky?

VLAD: Because that's what birds do.

VIORICA: Can I fly?

VLAD: No, you can't fly.

VIORICA: Why?

VLAD: Because you're not a bird. Only birds can fly.

VIORICA: Why?

VLAD: Because they have wings and you don't.

VIORICA: Why?

VLAD: Because you live on earth and birds live in the air.

VIORICA: Why can't I live in the air?

VLAD: Because you'd fall on the ground.

VIORICA: Why?

VLAD: Because…because…because you haven't got wings.

VIORICA: Why?

VLAD: Because you're a person and people don't have wings.

VIORICA puts her thumb in her mouth and stares at the sky. VLAD waits to see if she's going to ask any more questions. Just as he turns back to his gardening she speaks. ANA-MARIA is still listening.

VIORICA: My friend can fly.

VLAD: Can she?

VIORICA: It's not a she it's a he.

VLAD: Can he?

VIORICA: Yes. He's got wings.

VLAD: I see. Well he must be a very special kind of person.

VIORICA: He is.

ANA-MARIA: You shouldn't encourage her, Vlad.

VLAD: What's that, dear heart?

ANA-MARIA: Pretending you believe her. Don't be a silly little girl. Of course you haven't got a friend who can fly.

She closes the window. VLAD goes back to his garden.

VIORICA: Tatā?

VLAD: Yes, my sweetheart?

VIORICA: When will you take me to see the bears?

VLAD: One day, my love, one day. Once you're bigger and before I get too old.

SINGER: (*Sings.*)

IN THE SPRING THE CHERRY BLOSSOMS
DELIGHT US WITH THEIR FINERY.
SEE THE PETALS PINK AND PRETTY
ON THE LOVELY CHERRY TREE.

A GENTLE BREEZE BLOWS IN THE BRANCHES
AND THE PETALS FLUTTER DOWN.
IS IT SNOW? NO CHERRY FLOWERS!
LIKE A CARPET ON THE GROUND.

IN THE SUMMER SEE THE CHERRIES
RIPENING IN THE GOLDEN SUN.
BRING THE LADDER! HOLD THE BASKET!
BEFORE THE BIRDS EAT EVERY ONE.

IN THE AUTUMN, LEAVES ARE TURNING.
SOON THE BRANCHES WILL BE BARE.
WE WILL MAKE SWEET CHERRY BRANDY
STORE IT UNDERNEATH THE STAIR.

WHEN THE WINTER SNOW IS FALLING
FETCH THE BOTTLE, BRING THE GLASS!
LET US SIP THE SUMMER SUNSHINE
KNOWING WINTER TOO WILL PASS.

*During the song VLAD has to keep stopping VIORICA
pulling up flowers etc. He goes inside to put on his coat
and when he returns she has hidden. He rushes to look
for her and she emerges from her hiding place having
grown again. He leaves to go shopping.*

*VIORICA kneels at the window watching the snow.
She is now bigger.*

*VLAD enters with shopping bags and a gas bottle on
his back. He stamps his feet and coughs. ANA-MARIA
watches him.*

ANA-MARIA: You were a long time.

VLAD coughs again.

VIORICA: Tatā, did you get my sweets?

VLAD: Mmm?

ANA-MARIA: What's wrong with you?

VLAD: Nothing.

VIORICA: Tatā!

ANA-MARIA: Leave him!

VLAD: (*To VIORICA.*) What?

VIORICA: Did you get my sweets?

VLAD: Oh yes.

He reaches for his bag and nearly falls over.

ANA-MARIA: Nothing, eh? You'll go straight to bed.

She takes VLAD and lies him down.

The DOCTOR enters. ANA-MARIA sends VIORICA away. VIORICA tries to hear what they're saying.

DOCTOR: (*Looking in VLAD's mouth.*) Mmm.

ANA-MARIA looks at him.

(*Taking VLAD's pulse.*) Mmmmm.

ANA-MARIA looks at him again.

(*Listening to his chest.*) Mmmmmmmmm.

He packs his bag and takes out some pills.

He has a fever.

ANA-MARIA: I see.

DOCTOR: It's gone to his lungs.

ANA-MARIA: His lungs?

DOCTOR: Pneumonia.

ANA-MARIA: Pneumonia!

DOCTOR: Very serious at his age.

VIORICA gasps.

ANA-MARIA and the DOCTOR hear her and look. She hides.

Two of these four times a day and plenty of fluids.

ANA-MARIA: I see.

DOCTOR: Not that it will do much good.

Again VIORICA gasps.

I'll come back tomorrow.

ANA-MARIA: Thank you, Doctor.

He goes.

ANA-MARIA and VIORICA stand facing each other.

Get some water.

VIORICA goes to get a glass of water.

ANA-MARIA strokes VLAD's hair.

VIORICA enters and watches her.

What are you staring at, child? Here, give it to me.

She gives VLAD the pill.

(*To VIORICA.*) There's no need to look like that. You worried that you're going to be left here on you own with me? Is that it? You think I want that any more than you?

VIORICA goes.

ANA-MARIA strokes VLAD's hair.

VIORICA: (*Looking up.*) Where are you?
Hey!
Where are you?

ANA-MARIA gets up and overhears VIORICA.

Don't let him die!
Please don't let him die.

ANA-MARIA: How can he get better if you make such a racket? Go to sleep!

She goes back to VLAD.

VIORICA: (*Whispering.*) Where are you?
Where are you?

Heaven

GABRIEL enters. He sneezes.

GABRIEL: Alright, alright!
It's not funny.
You didn't know angels could get a cold, did you?
Neither did I!

He sneezes.

It's been freezing up here lately.
I was speaking to one of the older angels and he said he's
never known it so cold!
He says it's to do with something called global warming.
I told him if this is supposed to be global warming
Then it's not working!
I mean!
How would you like it?
We haven't got central heating up here, you know.

And no nice warm duvets.
Not like you.
These clouds might look pretty enough
But they're not much cop for keeping the chill out.

He sneezes.

And have you seen the clothes they give us to wear?
Look at this,
See how thin it is.
Oh yeah it looks nice enough
But that's the trouble with this get up you see
It's designed to look good when you're floating through
        the air
So that people go,
'Oooh, look at that angel
Isn't he beautiful?
All floaty and light.'

He sneezes.

But it doesn't keep you warm on a cold night.

ARCHANGEL GABRIEL: Gabriel!

GABRIEL: Oh no! What now?

He grabs his harp and tries to play it.

ARCHANGEL GABRIEL: Where are you Gabriel.

GABRIEL: I'm here your Celestial Majesty.

*GABRIEL is making the most dreadful noise on his
harp.*

ARCHANGEL GABRIEL: Not making much progress,
    are you?

GABRIEL: I haven't been feeling well.

ARCHANGEL GABRIEL: When were you last down
    there, Gabriel?

GABRIEL: I've had a terrible sore throat
And my nose has been –

ARCHANGEL GABRIEL: When, Gabriel?

GABRIEL: I was down there...
Let's see,
They were picking cherries
So it must have been last summer.
Or was it the summer before last?
That's the trouble with these seasons
They keep going round
And you start to lose count –

ARCHANGEL GABRIEL: The Old Man is ill, Gabriel.
He's been lying there for days.

GABRIEL: Oh dear.

ARCHANGEL GABRIEL: It's not time for him to come
up here yet.
Tell her
He'll be alright.

GABRIEL: Couldn't you get someone else to pass on the
message?
I'm really not feeling –

ARCHANGEL GABRIEL: Gabriel,
Don't you want those wings?

GABRIEL: Well, I...

ARCHANGEL GABRIEL: Go, Gabriel.

GABRIEL: Yes, oh Ineffable One.

Earth

*ANA-MARIA is asleep at VLAD's bedside. VIORICA too is
asleep.*

GABRIEL goes and looks at VLAD.

He sneezes.

VLAD and ANA-MARIA stir in their sleep. GABRIEL freezes.

They go back to sleep.

He moves on to VIORICA.

GABRIEL: He's dthoing to –

He suppresses a sneeze.

He's dthoing to be –

He takes out a handkerchief and blows his nose.

He's going to be alright.

VIORICA turns over and smiles in her sleep.

GABRIEL goes.

Birdsong.

ANA-MARIA goes to VLAD. There is a feather on VLAD's nose.

VLAD: Hello, my love.

ANA-MARIA: Vlad?

VLAD: Yes?

ANA-MARIA: Oh, Vlad, you're looking so much better.

The DOCTOR arrives and looks at VLAD.

He looks in his mouth.

DOCTOR: Hmmm.

He checks his pulse.

Hmmmmm.

He listens to his chest.

Hmmmmmm.

ANA-MARIA: Well?

DOCTOR: I don't understand.

ANA-MARIA: You don't?

DOCTOR: He's better.

ANA-MARIA: Yes.

DOCTOR: He's not supposed to be better.

ANA-MARIA: No?

DOCTOR: Dear me.

He goes.

More birdsong.

VLAD: Where's my Viorica?

ANA-MARIA: Sleeping.

VLAD sleeps.

ANA-MARIA strokes his hair.

ANA-MARIA: (*Sings.*)
DEAR ONE
DEAR HEART
WE WERE NEVER MEANT TO PART.
I CANNOT LIVE WITHOUT YOUR SMILE
I NEED YOU WITH ME ALL THE WHILE.

She goes and gets her photo album.

DEAR ONE
DEAREST LOVE
ANGELS LOOK DOWN FROM ABOVE.
LOOKED AT US SO JEALOUSLY.
CAME AND STOLE MY LOVE FROM ME.

Suddenly she looks up. VIORICA is standing there.

Come in. Don't stand there gawping.

VIORICA: Is tatā…?

ANA-MARIA: He's better.

VIORICA hugs ANA-MARIA.

(*Softer.*) Alright, alright.

She wipes VIORICA's eyes.

(*Looking at the photo. Sings.*)
DEAR ONE
DEAR HEART
WE WERE NEVER MEANT TO PART.
I'LL NEVER SEE YOUR SMILE AGAIN
I WAIT IN DARKNESS FOR MY END.

She lets VIORICA brush her hair. She hums the tune as she looks at the photo.

It is a moment of closeness and tenderness between them.

She turns the page of the album. Suddenly VIORICA notices the photo. She stops brushing.

Why have you stopped?

VIORICA: That's…

ANA-MARIA: What?

VIORICA: That's my friend.

ANA-MARIA: Don't start all that again, child.

VIORICA: It's him. It's him.

ANA-MARIA: You should have grown out of all that imaginary friend business by now.

VIORICA: But it's him. He comes to visit me.

ANA-MARIA: Don't tell lies now.

VIORICA: I'm not lying. He came to see me last night and told me –

ANA-MARIA snatches the hair-brush from her.

ANA-MARIA: Do you know what happens to little girls who tell lies?

VIORICA: But it's him.

ANA-MARIA: Listen to me! Vlad might think your stories about your friend are harmless but you're not going to get away with those games with me. You're a little liar. You're nobody, do you hear me? Some street person left you on our doorstep with that cheap and nasty ring round your neck. And you should thank your lucky stars that they happened to choose a house where a poor silly fool like Vlad was living. But you're still nobody. And you're not going to creep into my heart by making up stories about my beautiful boy.

She starts brushing her hair again.

Go on! Leave me!

VIORICA runs away in tears.

GABRIEL enters.

GABRIEL: Now, what's wrong?

VIORICA turns away from him.

Little girl.

She turns away from him again.

Hello!

He waves at her. She covers her eyes.

He flaps his wings at her.

VIORICA: Go away.

He tickles her with a feather.

Stop it. You don't exist.

GABRIEL: What do you mean?

VIORICA: You're not real.

GABRIEL: But I'm here.

VIORICA: No, you're not. So go away.

GABRIEL: How can I go away if I'm not here?

VIORICA: Because I made you up.

GABRIEL: No you didn't.

VIORICA: Yes, I did. I must have seen your photo and so
I made you up.

GABRIEL: My photo?

VIORICA: She's got your photo in her book
She said you're her son.

GABRIEL: Her son?

VIORICA: Yes.
I wanted a friend
So I pretended you were my friend.

GABRIEL: I am your friend.

VIORICA: No you're not.

GABRIEL: Little girl –

VIORICA: I never want to see you again.
Go away!
And never come back.

She hides under the bedclothes crying.

GABRIEL goes to ANA-MARIA. He looks at the photo.

GABRIEL: But that's…
   That's…
   Oh my…
   That's…
   It says underneath,
   'Gaby, Aged twenty-one.'
   That means
   I'm her…
   I'm their Gaby.
   She's my mother.
   They should have told me.
   (*Looking up.*) Why didn't you tell me?
   I don't want her for my mother.
   I don't like her.

   He goes.

   VLAD enters with his rucksack on.

VLAD: Viorica, are you ready?

VIORICA: (*Off.*) I'm coming.

   ANA-MARIA watches.

VLAD: I wish you were coming with us, my love.

ANA-MARIA: I don't like the countryside. You know that.
   What's there to do in the mountains? Every summer
   you made Gaby go with you to the mountains. He
   wanted to stay home and practice his violin. He hated
   the mountains. He was scared of the bears.

   VIORICA enters with a rucksack as well.

VLAD: All set? We'll miss our train. Goodbye my love.

   *ANA-MARIA puts up her cheek to be kissed. He kisses
   her.*

   Say goodbye to Aunty, Viorica.

ANA-MARIA: I'm not her aunty.

VIORICA goes to kiss her. ANA-MARIA avoids the kiss.

They go. ANA-MARIA walks back to the house. Suddenly she doubles up with pain.

A toy train crosses at the back of the stage.

SINGER: (*Sings.*)
OUT OF THE CITY
THROUGH THE PLAIN
UP INTO THE HILLS
GOES THE EXPRESS TRAIN
THROUGH THE WINDOW
WATCH THE VILLAGES GO PAST!
SEE THE CHILDREN WAVE
AS WE GO BY SO FAST.
HIGHER AND HIGHER WE GO
PAST WATERFALLS AND TREES.
DEER GRAZE IN THE FOREST.
BIRDS FLOAT ON THE BREEZE.
NOW WE SEE THE MOUNTAINS
THEIR TOPS STILL WHITE WITH SNOW
'WILL WE SEE A BEAR, TATĀ?'
'MY DEAR, YOU NEVER KNOW!'

VLAD and VIORICA sit beside their camp fire at night. Stars come out. Calls of night animals and birds.

VIORICA: Tatā?

VLAD: Yes, my dear?

VIORICA: I think I might be a bit scared of bears.

VLAD: No need to be scared, my darling.

VIORICA: Would a bear hurt me?

VLAD: If you frightened it, it might. Or if it was a she bear with its cubs.

VIORICA: Why?

VLAD: Because the Mummy bear will do anything to protect its little one.

The moon rises. VIORICA takes the ring from around her neck and looks at it.

VIORICA: Tatā?

VLAD: Yes, my sweet?

VIORICA: Where do you think my Mummy is?

VLAD: I don't know, darling. But wherever she is, I'm sure she's thinking about you. Look it fits your middle finger.

He puts the ring on her finger.

A roar in the distance. VLAD looks.

VIORICA: Can you see a bear, tatā?

VLAD: I can see two!

VIORICA is alarmed.

VIORICA: Two!

VLAD: Yes.

VIORICA: Where?

She peers into the darkness.

Is that one over there?

VLAD: No, that's my rucksack lying in the grass.

VIORICA: There?

VLAD: No, that's a rock down by the stream.

VIORICA: There?

VLAD: No, that's a wild raspberry bush.

VIORICA: Where then?

VLAD: Up there.

He point to the sky.

Can you see the seven stars up there?

VIORICA: Where?

VLAD: There. Follow my finger. That's the Great Bear. You see it?

VIORICA: Yes.

VLAD: And there, just above it, there are six stars making two legs and a neck. Much smaller.

VIORICA: Yes.

VLAD: That's the Little Bear.

VIORICA: Oh.

VLAD: And all through time they chase each other across the sky.

VIORICA: And do they ever catch each other?

VLAD: No, they never do.

VIORICA: Why not?

VLAD: Because many millions of years ago before any of this was here, there was a big explosion that sent all the stars and planets spinning away from each other. All the time they get further and further apart.

VIORICA: For ever and ever?

VLAD: No not forever. One day it will all get smaller again. Maybe then the Great Bear will gather the Little Bear in its arms again.

VIORICA: I hope so tatā.

She looks at the ring on her finger. She yawns.

VLAD: Time for bed, sweetheart.

He picks her up and takes her indoors.

A big starry bear chases a little starry bear across the sky.

Heaven

ARCHANGEL GABRIEL: Gabriel!

A little cloud shuffles away slightly.

Come on, Gabriel, you can't sulk in that cloud forever.

The little cloud shuffles a bit more.

Alright, I should have told you.

The cloud nods its head.

Gabriel! You're not going to make me say sorry,
are you?

The cloud nods its head even more vigorously.

An archangel never says sorry.

The cloud shrugs its shoulders and turns its back.

Alright, Gabriel, I'm sorry. Satisfied?

The cloud indicates that it's not sure.

Look, Gabriel. Usually we don't tell angels about
their past lives. We think it confuses things. They start
thinking about the past instead of getting on with their
jobs looking after people and such.

The cloud turns its back again.

*In the next section we see small puppet versions of
VLAD, ANA-MARIA and GABY act out the story as
the archangel tells it.*

They loved you very much, your parents, the two old

fogeys as you call them. But they couldn't agree what was best for you. Your father, Vlad loved the country of your birth. He used to take you walking in the mountains and the forests. He wanted you to love it like him. But your mother wanted you to be a great musician.

The cloud looks at him in surprise.

Yes, a musician. She told you about cities in far-away lands where you could study and learn. So you decided to leave. You didn't like the mountains and you were always scared of the bears. So one day they took you to the airport and you got on the aeroplane and flew far away.

GABRIEL has poked his head out of the cloud to listen.

But you weren't used to those places. The streets were crowded and there were so many cars. You suddenly missed the mountains and the forests. One day you were out in the street and you saw a bird way up in the sky. It was a big bird like the birds of the mountains. So you were looking up in the sky and you weren't looking where you were going. You didn't see the car coming towards you on the left hand side of the road.

GABRIEL: And I was killed.

ARCHANGEL GABRIEL: Yes, you were killed.

GABRIEL says nothing.

It was very sad.

Still he says nothing.

And your parents were very sad.

Still nothing.

That's why your mother never smiled or sang again. Look at her down there.

ANA-MARIA paces up and down at night. She is in pain.

She is ill, Gabriel. It will soon be time for her to die. When that time comes you must go to her.

GABRIEL looks at ANA-MARIA.

But before then, you have to go one more time to the little girl.

GABRIEL: The little girl!
She doesn't like me any more.
Didn't you hear her?
I thought you saw everything.
She said she never wants to see me again.

ARCHANGEL GABRIEL: But she needs you, Gabriel.
One last time.

GABRIEL: Where is she?

ARCHANGEL GABRIEL: In the forest.

GABRIEL: The forest?

ARCHANGEL GABRIEL: Yes, the forest.

GABRIEL: You mean where there's –

He mimes a bear rising on its paws as at the beginning.

Where there's –

He mimes a bear snarling.

ARCHANGEL GABRIEL: Yes, Gabriel
You have to be very brave.

GABRIEL: I'm not a very brave person –
I mean angel.

ARCHANGEL GABRIEL: You don't know that.
Will you go to her, Gabriel?

GABRIEL: I don't know.

ARCHANGEL GABRIEL: Don't you want wings like mine?

GABRIEL: No.

ARCHANGEL GABRIEL: You've got to go to her, Gabriel,

GABRIEL: Say please.

ARCHANGEL GABRIEL: An archangel never says please.

GABRIEL turns away.

Alright, please.

GABRIEL turns to him.

GABRIEL: I'll think about it.

He gets back in his cloud.

Earth

Sound of bees. VIORICA runs on and hides.

VLAD enters.

VLAD: Viorica?

She makes the sound of a bear.

I think there's a bear around here.

She makes the sound again.

Hope it likes sandwiches with honey!

She pounces on him. He pretends to be frightened.

She takes the sandwich.

VIORICA: Look, tatā.

VLAD: Yes.
It's a pool of water.

They look in the pond.

VIORICA: Look!
Hello, little girl.

VLAD: She's waving at you.

VIORICA: Hello.

VLAD: (*Waving.*) Hello.

VIORICA: The man's waving. Hello.

VLAD: Hello.

VIORICA: He's waving again.
Look, tatā,
The little girl has got a sandwich just like me.

VLAD: So she has.

VIORICA: (*Loudly, to her reflection.*) I've got one too.

VLAD: I wonder what their lives are like down there under
the water. Do you think it's any better than ours?

VIORICA: They're not really there.
It's just a reflection.

VLAD: Oh, of course.

VIORICA: Silly.

She yawns.

VLAD: The little girl's tired.
She wants a rest.

VIORICA falls asleep by the pool.

VLAD lies down some distance away.

Sound of bees and the breeze in the branches; scratchings

and shufflings; twigs cracking and fallen leaves rustling; of grasses being pushed aside and fur brushing against tree trunks. VLAD and VIORICA respond in their sleep but do not wake. As they sleep more deeply the light gets darker. There is just one shaft of light on VIORICA.

A BEAR CUB enters and looks at her. He sniffs at her face and hands. She bats it away as if it were a bee.

There is a growl. The little BEAR CUB looks up.

A huge BEAR enters and moves towards her cub and VIORICA.

It growls.

VLAD wakes up. He turns and sees the BEAR near VIORICA. He knows that he must not move.

The BEAR rears on its hind legs and growls again. VLAD looks around for a branch or a weapon but there is nothing.

GABRIEL appears in a shaft of light. He has his harp and is suddenly able to play it.

The BEAR roars.

GABRIEL stands his ground and the music continues.

Suddenly the BEAR sinks on all fours, turns heel and disappears, the BEAR CUB scampering after it.

VLAD looks at the angel.

Gaby?

GABRIEL: It's alright, tatā.
Everything is alright.

VIORICA wakes up.

VIORICA: You came back.

GABRIEL: Yes.

He disappears into the darkness.

VLAD rushes over to VIORICA and holds her,

VIORICA: That was my friend.
Did you see him, tatā?

VLAD: Yes, my dear.
I saw him.

They get up and leave.

The train goes back down the mountain.

ANA-MARIA is in bed. The DOCTOR comes to visit her.

DOCTOR: Where does it hurt?

ANA-MARIA: Here.

DOCTOR: *(Feeling her.)* Mmm.

ANA-MARIA: And here.

DOCTOR: Mmmmm.

ANA-MARIA: And here.

DOCTOR: Mmmmmmmm.

ANA-MARIA: I think I ate too many radishes last night.

DOCTOR: Radishes. Mmmmmmmmmm.

VLAD enters with VIORICA.

VLAD: Ana-Maria!

ANA-MARIA: What's wrong with me, Doctor?

DOCTOR: There's nothing wrong with you.

VLAD: Ana-Maria, where are you? We're back.

He comes into the room.

What's wrong?

ANA-MARIA: There's nothing wrong, is there, Doctor?

DOCTOR: Nothing at all. You've years ahead of you. Fit as a fiddle, you are.

VLAD: She looks so ill.

DOCTOR: Your wife just has a touch of indigestion, Sir. Give her one of these if it continues.

VLAD: But –

DOCTOR: Hmmmmm.

He goes.

VIORICA: Shall we tell her about the bear, tatā?

VLAD: No, my sweet.
You go and unpack while I look after Aunty.

VIORICA goes.

ANA-MARIA winces in pain.

Ana-Maria.

He strokes her hair.

(*Sings.*)
DEAR ONE, DEAR HEART
YOU AND I SHOULD NEVER PART.
DEAREST MINE, DEAR LOVE
ANGELS LOOK DOWN FROM ABOVE.

VIORICA: Tatā, there was a letter in the box.

VLAD: A letter?

She gives it to him.

From Italy. Who do we know in Italy?

ANA-MARIA: What are you talking about?

VLAD: There's a letter here from Milan.

ANA-MARIA: Why don't you open it and see?

VIORICA: Can I have the stamp, tatā?

ANA-MARIA: Keep the child away from me, Vlad.

VLAD: Here you are my love. Go and put it in your album.

He gives the stamp to her and she goes.

VLAD opens the letter and reads. During the letter two puppets representing GABY and the MOTHER act out the story of their courtship, his departure and death, her leaving the baby and working in Italy.

VLAD: Dear Sir and Madam,

MOTHER: Dear Sir and Madam,

You don't know me but I was a friend of your son, Gaby, before he went away. I write 'friend' but as you will realise from reading this letter, we were much more to each other than friends. He wanted me to meet you but you should know that my own parents were both dead and I was just a poor girl. So we decided to wait until he came back from abroad. But I loved your son and when I heard about his death I wanted to die too.

GABRIEL enters and listens to the letter.

Then I realised I was having his baby. Dear Sir and Madam, please don't think badly of me. I didn't know what to do for the best. Perhaps I should have to come to you for help but I was too scared. Gaby was so clever and I knew that you would think I was not good enough for him. But then I was offered work here in Italy. What was I to do? I couldn't take my baby with me to Italy. I believed you would not want the child if you knew I was her mother. So I left her on your doorstep. I thought it was for the best. On a chain around her neck I put the ring that Gaby gave me before he went away.

GABRIEL goes and looks at VIORICA who is sticking the stamp into her album.

There has not been a day when I have not thought about my baby and I have sat down to write this letter many times. All I ask is that you find it in your heart to forgive me. And maybe one day you will let me meet my daughter so that I can put right the wrong I did by abandoning her.

GABRIEL touches VIORICA's head.

VLAD and ANA-MARIA look at each other.

VLAD: She's our granddaughter, Ana-Maria. Our Gaby's daughter.

ANA-MARIA: Too late.

VLAD: What's too late?

ANA-MARIA: The letter. It came too late.

VLAD: No.

ANA-MARIA: Not for you. But too late for me.

VLAD: Viorica!

VIORICA approaches fearfully.

ANA-MARIA looks at her.

ANA-MARIA: She has his eyes.

She reaches out and takes VIORICA's hand. She looks at the ring on her finger.

Viorica.

A spasm grips her. She turns her head away and motions for them to leave.

VLAD and VIORICA go.

The light gets brighter on ANA-MARIA.

GABRIEL walks into the light. His wings are huge.

Gaby. My Gaby. I've missed you so.

GABRIEL: I've been here all the time, Mother. Couldn't you hear me when the birds sang in the cherry tree in Spring? Couldn't you taste me in the brandy father made in autumn or feel my warm breath on your hand when the winds blew from Siberia in winter?

ANA-MARIA: When you died I didn't let myself hear or smell or taste or feel ever again.

GABRIEL: So you couldn't see me, Mother, looking out at you from my child's eyes.

He goes and touches her face.

ANA-MARIA: That feels better.

GABRIEL: Come, Mother.

He gathers her in his arms and lifts her away on wings of gold.

The sound of a violin.

VLAD stands looking at the photo album. VIORICA calls.

VIORICA: Tată, come on, we'll be late for the train.

VLAD: I'm coming, I'm coming.

VIORICA: I think I can hear it.

VLAD: She'll wait for us, don't worry my sweet.

Sound of train approaching.

VIORICA: Do you think she'll like me, tatā?

VLAD: Of course she'll like you, little one.

The sound of the train gets nearer.

VIORICA: Is my hat straight, tatā?

VLAD: You look lovely.

Sound of train pulling up.

Noise of people getting off.

The VIORICA puppet is looking for her mother.

There she is.

VIORICA: I'm scared, tatā.

VLAD: Don't be scared, my little violet.

The VIORICA puppet starts to walk. She seems to be walking without being manipulated. She stands alone in a huge universe.

VIORICA: I'm here. I'm here.

The stars appear in the sky. The Great Bear and The Little Bear embrace.

The End.

WWW.OBERONBOOKS.COM

Follow us on www.twitter.com/@oberonbooks
& www.facebook.com/oberonbook

9 781840 022179